Contents

Words printed in bold letters, **like these**,
are explained in the Glossary.

How artists see families

The Painter's Family by Henri Matisse, 1911

For hundreds of years, artists have painted and taken photographs of families. Sometimes the artists were trying to show how important a family was. At other times, the paintings and photographs were made just so people would be able to remember their families growing up. Here Matisse has painted his own family in their home. The children are playing a board game.

When the first camera was invented in 1827 it took over eight hours to take a photograph. It would have been very expensive and only wealthy people could have recorded their families in this way. By the time the **Victorian** family above had their picture taken, cameras were a bit easier and cheaper to use.

Digital snaps

This colour photograph is very modern. It shows a family from our century. It was taken with a **digital camera**. The electronic image can be stored on a **CD-ROM** or even posted on a family website.

Using line

This picture was painted over 2000 years before cameras were invented. It shows people of different ages who look like each other. They were probably members of the same family from a place called **Corinth**. The people are drawn with line and then painted with blocks of **primary colours**. The figures are drawn from the side. The whole image looks very flat.

Corinthian plaque from Pitsa, Greece, around 540 BC

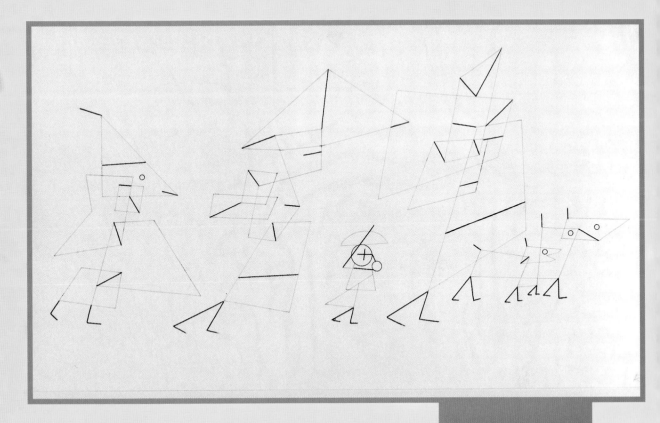

This family is also drawn from the side using line. This time the figures are not coloured in. The shapes are all lopsided triangles, rectangles and semi-circles. Paul Klee thought hard about which shapes looked most like the different parts of the body. Do you think he got it right?

Using colour

Here Georges Seurat has painted families enjoying a Sunday afternoon together. Instead of mixing all his colours on his **palette**, the artist placed dots of different colours next to each other on the **canvas**. When our eyes see these colours together our brains mix them up so we see other colours. This gives the painting a sunny, hazy feel.

A Sunday Afternoon on the Island of La Grande Jatte by Georges Seurat, 1884–86.

Pissarro has painted families going to an exhibition in a big glass building in London. Look at how he only uses blocks of colour to show their clothes and their hair. We can see lots of people walking away from us. Perhaps the artist wanted us to think we could follow them on their day out.

Bold shapes

The clothes the family are wearing in this picture are made up of different patterns. The basic shapes of the clothes are cut out and then arranged on the picture. We call this a **montage**. A montage can be made using scissors, paper and glue. It can also be done on a computer.

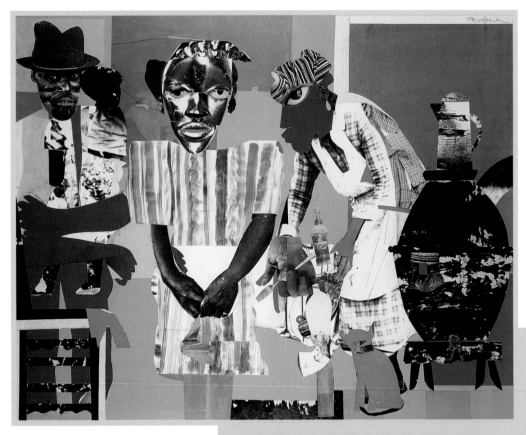

Sunday Morning Breakfast by Romare Howard Bearden, 1967

The first steps
by Pablo
Picasso, 1943

Pablo Picasso also used basic shapes in this picture of a mother and her son. First he drew the mother and son from different angles. Then he mixed the drawings together to make an **abstract** picture. The shapes are like jigsaw pieces. They fit together to show the mother and son holding each other closely.

11

A family likeness

Isaac Winslow and His Family
by Joseph Blackburn, 1755

People belonging to the same family tend to look alike. Look at the people in this painting. The artist has painted their faces in a lot of detail, to help show how similar they look.

This family have had their group **portrait** taken by a photographer. They chose to have the picture taken at a beautiful spot in Japan, where they live. See how each member of the family looks similar. Do you look like people in your family?

The Shimada Family by Thomas Struth, 1986.

Painting people

It takes a long time to paint a **portrait** like this. In the eighteenth century artists used dolls to replace the people for some of the time. This may be why these two people seem to be a bit stiff! Thomas Gainsborough only really needed to see Heneage Lloyd and his sister when he painted their faces.

Heneage Lloyd and his Sister by Thomas Gainsborough, mid-1750s

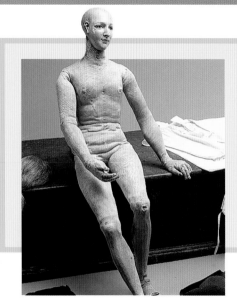

Artists' dolls
Artists' dolls like this one were used by eighteenth-century artists. They showed the artist what people looked like when they were sitting or standing.

Mr and Mrs Clark and Percy
by David Hockney, 1970

Mr and Mrs Clark probably **posed** at different times for their portraits. Percy the cat would have found it more difficult to stay still! *Mr and Mrs Clark and Percy* and *Heneage Lloyd and his Sister* were painted more than 200 years apart. From the portraits we can see how differently they lived and how fashions have changed over the years.

Giving people form

Did you know?

Many artists use a layer of green paint underneath flesh colours to make people look more real. Joshua Reynolds never finished this painting. This means that we can see how the layers of paint were built up.

When Sir Joshua Reynolds painted this **portrait** he would have placed the people near a window. This would have made it easier for him to see the light and dark tones. Shadows and highlights give flat paintings the feeling of **depth**. This woman and her daughter are painted looking straight towards us. The light shining on their faces makes them look **three-dimensional**.

This odd-looking sculpture of a **pregnant** woman really is three-dimensional. You can walk all the way around it. It was made by **welding** pieces of metal together. The simple shapes of the pieces work together to make a very interesting **abstract** figure.

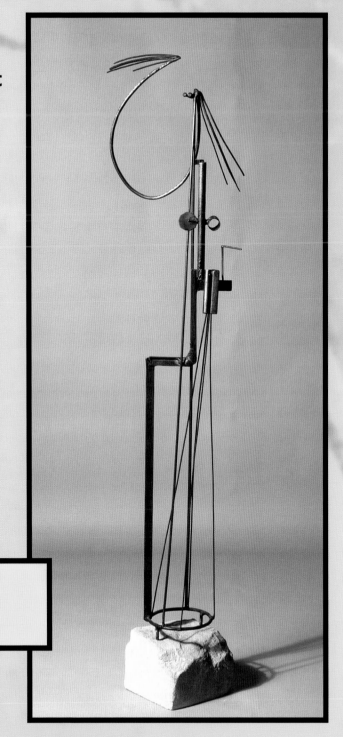

Maternity by Julio Gonzalez, 1934

Measuring heads and bodies

When artists draw or make sculptures of people they use the head as a unit of measurement. Count how many times the little dancer's head fits into the whole length of her body. It should be about seven times.

Little Dancer Aged Fourteen by Edgar Degas, around 1920–21

Ghost by Ron Mueck, 1998

It is quite difficult to measure the height of the girl in Ron Mueck's sculpture because she is leaning against a wall. The sculpture is much bigger than a real-life girl, however her head is still the right size compared to her body. We say it is in **proportion**.

How artists measure heads and bodies

Try this technique for measuring people like artists do:

1 Place a pencil in your hand.
2 Hold your arm out straight.
3 Line the tip of the pencil with the top of the person's head.
4 Mark the bottom of the head with your thumb.
5 Using the space between the tip of the pencil and your thumb, measure how many times it would fit in to the full length of the person's body.
6 You can now use this measurement to draw a person in proportion. The number of times the person's head would fit in to the length of their body is the number of times bigger you should draw their body compared to their head!

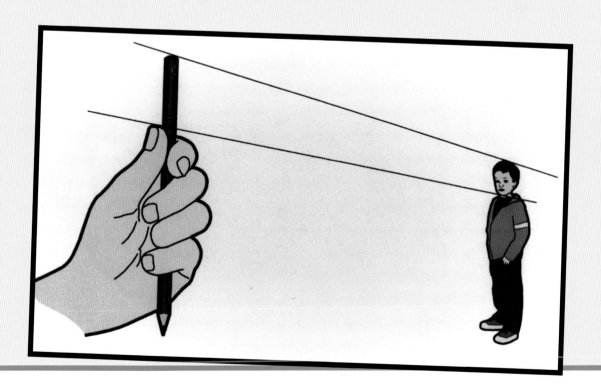

Drawing children

The Graham Children by William Hogarth, 1742

The children in this picture look quite grown up in their posh clothes. In the eighteenth century, children were dressed to look like small adults. The baby is wearing a dress, but it isn't a little girl. In those days, baby boys wore dresses too!

Mary Cassatt's painting shows a mother washing her child. Look at how large the child's head is, compared to her body. Like all young animals, human children look cute. This makes people want to look after them. Count how many times the child's head fits in to the length of her body. It is much less than a teenager or an adult.

The Bath by Mary Cassatt, around 1891

Cartoon babies

In cartoons, babies' heads are made even larger than in real life. This is why we find them so sweet. Their big eyes and chubby faces make them look even cuter than normal.

A *still* from the Rugrats cartoon

Expressing emotions

Here we see people watching a man explaining how the **solar system** works. The children's expressions show they are fascinated. Joseph Wright used friends and their families to **pose** in many of his paintings. We do not know who the children in this picture are, but it is likely that they are brother and sister. This is because their faces are quite similar.

The Orrery by Joseph Wright of Derby, around 1764–66

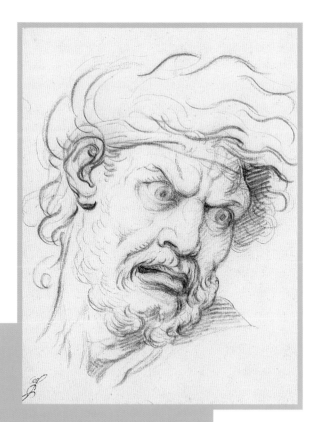

Charles Le Brun made these diagrams using just lines and tone to show what happens to people's faces when they make different expressions. Look at how the eyes, nose and mouth all change.

Anger by Charles Le Brun, around 1668

Laughter by Charles Le Brun, around 1668

Try this!

Try using simple lines to draw faces that look:
- happy
- sad
- angry
- thoughtful.

Painting older people

Portrait of the Artist's Parents
by Otto Dix, 1924

When we age our faces change. Our skin becomes wrinkled and less firm. This painting shows older people. In the painting, the artist has used lines and shadows to make the people's faces look older.

What will you look like when you are older?

You will need:

- a close-up photograph of your face
- a close-up photograph of an older relative's face
- tracing paper
- a soft pencil.

Instructions:

1 Find two similar-sized close-up photographs of your face and the face of an older relative. If you cannot find any suitable photographs, you could ask someone to use a camera to take some for you.

2 Place tracing paper over the photograph of your older family member. Now trace the lines on their face using a soft pencil.

3 Lay the tracing on top of the photograph of yourself. You should now be able to see what you might look like when you get older!

Royal family portraits

Famous people, like kings and queens, paid artists to make them look wealthy and powerful. Here, the **Tudor** kings Henry VII and his son Henry VIII are shown in their fine clothes. Henry VIII is **posing** in the **foreground**, making him look even more important. He also looks very heavy. Being heavy in the sixteenth century meant that you were wealthy, because you could afford to eat plenty of rich food.

Henry VII and Henry VIII by Hans Holbein the Younger, around 1536–37

An ancient portrait
This portrait was found in a **tomb** in Egypt. It was made thousands of years ago, in about 1340 BC. The picture shows the Ancient Egyptian king, Tutankhamen, sitting with his wife.

Today kings and queens are not so powerful. This **portrait** of the British royal family shows them relaxing together, more like a normal family. They are in a very grand room at Buckingham Palace.

The Royal Family: A Centenary Portrait by John Wonnacott, 2000

Did you notice?

Did you notice how Prince Charles (right) and Prince William (left), the heirs to the throne, are in the foreground? This is to make them seem important.

The wedding album

The Peasant Wedding by Pieter Brueghel the Elder, 1568

Weddings are special occasions when family and friends get together. Pieter Brueghel's painting shows us a wedding feast where everyone is having fun. He has packed lots of people in to the **composition**. The whole painting is full of characters doing different things.

Bride and Groom by Amadeo Modigliani, 1915–16

This **portrait** of a bride and groom could have been painted to remind them of their big day. Even though it looks like a traditional **formal** painting, the artist has painted the bride and groom in his own style. Look how Modigliani has made the faces very long.

29

Glossary

abstract   art not meant to look like real life, but which shows feelings or an idea

canvas   cloth material that many artists use to paint on

CD-ROM   form of storage used to store computer data

composition   how a painting is put together

Corinth   a place in ancient Greece

depth   feeling of space and distance in a picture

digital camera   camera that stores photos electronically instead of using film

foreground   the part of a picture that looks the closest

formal   carried out in a traditional way

montage   picture that is put together by arranging together different pieces of material

palette   tool used by artists to mix paint on

portrait   painting or photograph of a real person

pose   when someone puts themselves in a particular position in order to be drawn

pregnant   when a woman has a baby growing inside her

primary colours   the three colours that cannot be mixed from other colours: red, blue and yellow

proportion   an object's size compared to another object

solar system   group of planets that go round the sun

still   photograph taken from a film

three-dimensional   when an object has height, width and depth

tomb   place where dead people are buried

Tudor   the name of an English royal family which ruled from 1485 to 1603

Victorian   from the reign of British Queen Victoria, 1837–1901

weld   join pieces of metal by melting them together

Finding out more

More books to read

Heinemann Library's *How Artists Use* series:

- *Colour*
- *Line and Tone*
- *Pattern and Texture*
- *Perspective*
- *Shape*

Heinemann Library's *The Life and Work of* series:

- *Auguste Rodin*
- *Barbara Hepworth*
- *Buonarroti Michelangelo*
- *Claude Monet*
- *Edgar Degas*
- *Georges Seurat*
- *Henri Matisse*
- *Henry Moore*
- *Joseph Turner*
- *Leonardo Da Vinci*
- *Mary Cassatt*
- *Paul Cezanne*
- *Paul Gauguin*
- *Paul Klee*
- *Pieter Breugel*
- *Rembrandt van Rijn*
- *Vincent Van Gogh*
- *Wassily Kandinsky*

Websites to visit

www.eurogallery.org – this website lets you search the art collections of important museums and galleries across the whole of Europe.

www.nationalgallery.org.uk – this is the website of the National Gallery in London. All of the works in the collection can be seen online.

Index